I0605815

THE LITTLE BOOK OF
LAS VEGAS

Copyright © 2026 Headline Publishing Group Limited

The right of Malcolm Croft to be identified as the Author of the Work has been asserted by him in accordance with the Copyright, Designs and Patents Act 1988.

First published in 2026 by OH
An Imprint of HEADLINE PUBLISHING GROUP LIMITED

1

Disclaimer:
All trademarks, copyright, quotations, company names, registered names, products, characters, logos and catchphrases used or cited in this book are the property of their respective owners.

Apart from any use permitted under UK copyright law, this publication may only be reproduced, stored, or transmitted, in any form, or by any means, with prior permission in writing of the publishers or, in the case of reprographic production, in accordance with the terms of licences issued by the Copyright Licensing Agency.

Cataloguing in Publication Data is available from the British Library

ISBN 978-1-03543-483-1

Compiled and written by Malcolm Croft
Editorial: Stella Caldwell
Designed and typeset in Joanna Nova by Stephen Cary
Project manager: Russell Porter
Production: Marion Storz
Printed and bound in Dubai

Headline's policy is to use papers that are natural, renewable and recyclable products and made from wood grown in well-managed forests and other controlled sources. The logging and manufacturing processes are expected to conform to the environmental regulations of the country of origin.

HEADLINE PUBLISHING GROUP LIMITED
An Hachette UK Company
Carmelite House, 50 Victoria Embankment, London EC4Y 0DZ

The authorised representative in the EEA is Hachette Ireland, 8 Castlecourt Centre, Dublin 15, D15 XTP3, Ireland (email: info@hbgi.ie)

www.headline.co.uk www.hachette.co.uk

THE LITTLE BOOK OF

LAS VEGAS

BIGGER, LOUDER & BRIGHTER

CONTENTS

INTRODUCTION – 6

8 CHAPTER ONE — ROLL THE DICE

38 CHAPTER TWO — CITY OF SIN

68 CHAPTER THREE — NEON PARADISE

98 CHAPTER FOUR — STRIP TEASE

128 CHAPTER FIVE — DESERT OASIS

158 CHAPTER SIX — VIVA LAS VEGAS

INTRODUCTION

Welcome to fabulous Lost Wages – sorry, Las Vegas. It's a city as beguiling as it is bonkers, as glamorous as it is gaudy and as decadent as it is, well, outrageous. *All at the same time.* Judging by the Strip's sheer love of excess – and the staggering number of visitors it draws every single year – one thing is resoundingly clear: Las Vegas always bets big on spectacle, style and sheer audacity. And we love every wild, glittering moment of it.

This little guide to the original Sin City is the ultimate celebration of Earth's brightest – and, paradoxically, darkest – city. A place filled with winners and losers, high rollers and low-ballers, magic and disillusion – all on such an epic, overwhelming scale, it makes its neighbouring landmark, the

Grand Canyon, seem tiny by comparison!

Inside you'll meet mobsters and movie stars, showgirls and playboys, and a dazzling detonation of indulgence and decadence. It's the famed city that never sleeps (even though it boasts an abundance of hotel bedrooms) – a place built to tempt, thrill and whet your appetite for your own unforgettable Vegas story. Because, let's face it, you haven't lived until you've gambled more than you can afford on the Strip. That's just the Vegas way, baby.

So, forget your fear and loathing – it's time to go all-in! Who knows what Lady Luck has in store for us? Just remember, what happens in Vegas, stays in Vegas – and that goes double for your money.

Please enjoy… responsibly!

CHAPTER ONE

Roll the Dice

It's time to spin the wheel of fortune, pull the lever of destiny and roll the dice of chance.

The lights are flashing, the stakes are high – and the possibilities? Endless.

So, what do you reckon – are you feeling lucky?

“

What you need is a weekend in Las Vegas, the playground of the world.

”

Tom Cassidy, *Psycho*, 1960

May 15, 1905

Las Vegas's birthday! It was on this date the San Pedro, Los Angeles and Salt Lake Railroad was completed, forging a crucial link between Southern California and Salt Lake City and establishing Las Vegas as a railroad town.

Today, it features a monorail and has played a key role in early Hyperloop development – becoming the first U.S. city to host a test track.

6.8 km*

The total length of the Las Vegas Strip.

It's the equivalent of almost 62 American football fields!

*4.2 miles

What happens in Vegas… stays in Vegas

Las Vegas's legendary motto was created in 2003 by the Las Vegas Convention and Visitors Authority (LVCVA) and the advertising agency R&R Partners. The goal was to brand the city as a tourist hotspot for "adult freedom".

The slogan remains a cultural phenomenon. "Tourists actually believe it when they go to Las Vegas," ad man Jason Hoff said of his creation.

Originating in Quebec in 1984, Cirque du Soleil revolutionized circus arts with its stylish acrobatic performances across a multitude of Vegas shows.

The company first landed on the Strip in 1993 with *Mystère* at Treasure Island. Today, more than 100 million visitors have seen a Cirque du Soleil show in Las Vegas.

Since 1952, more than 85 Hollywood films have been set in Las Vegas.

These are the most iconic - do you have a favourite?

1. *Viva Las Vegas* (1964)
2. *Diamonds Are Forever* (1971)
3. *Fear and Loathing in Las Vegas* (1998)
4. *Casino* (1995)
5. *Ocean's Eleven* (2001)
6. *The Hangover* (2009)
7. *Leaving Las Vegas* (1995)
8. *Rain Man* (1988)
9. *Swingers* (1996)
10. *Showgirls* (1995)
11. *Honeymoon in Vegas* (1992)
12. *Austin Powers: International Man of Mystery* (1997)

165 metres*

The height of the Eiffel Tower at the Paris Las Vegas Hotel & Casino – making it one of the city's biggest landmarks.

Built in 1999, it is precisely half the length of the real Eiffel Tower in Paris, France.

Visitors can ride an elevator all the way to the top.

*541 feet

October 3, 2003

The infamous night that Mantecore, a 172-kg (380-pound) white tiger and star of the legendary Siegfried & Roy illusionist act, attacked Roy Horn during a sold-out performance at the Mirage in front of 1,500 guests.

There was a lot of blood.

Often voted as one of the best swimming pools in the world – a prestigious honour for Vegas, the home of the pool party! – Mandalay Bay Beach is a 45,000-square-metre (11-acre) "aquatic playground".

The man-made beach was built using 2,700 tonnes of real sand while the wave pool holds over 6 million litres (1.6 million gallons) of water.

Who fancies a lounge in the lagoon?

Luxor's the Blue Man Group debuted in Las Vegas in 2000, arguably giving the city its most batshit crazy show!

Performed by three bald, blue and silent figures, the Blue Man Group has entertained more than 35 million fans and remains one of the top family-friendly acts in a city full of sin.

If you go, prepare to get messy with paint!

Las Vegas is the only place in the world where you can take a selfie with an ancient Egyptian pyramid, a Medieval English castle, the New York skyline and the Eiffel Tower all in the background.

No trip to the Strip is complete without visiting a gift shop and buying a one-of-a-kind kitschy souvenir.

Naturally, Las Vegas is home to Bonanza, touted as the largest (and weirdest!) gift shop in the world – about 3,700 square metres (40,000 square feet).

If you go, get the grass flip-flops.

Icons of Las Vegas: Howard Hughes

In November 1966, American aviation engineer and billionaire Howard Hughes moved into the Desert Inn – and stayed for four years. When asked to leave, he simply bought the hotel – and many others.

Within a few years, he became Nevada's largest private employer, casino owner and property owner, ushering in Vegas's Golden Age.

Thirteen of the 20 biggest hotels in the U.S. are in Las Vegas. And they say 13 is unlucky?

The Venetian Las Vegas and the Palazzo, operating together as the Venetian Complex with more than 7,000 rooms, form the second-largest hotel in the world – right after the First World Hotel in Malaysia.

Meanwhile, the MGM Grand, located at the southern end of the Strip, proudly holds the title of the third-largest hotel.

Las Vegas is the home of the epic pool party. The best? Head to the Encore Beach Club at Wynn, voted the top "Adult Party Pool".

Every day, a world-famous club DJ or musical act provides a soundtrack of up-tempo tracks to keep your poolside downtime vibrant and alive.

Just remember – please act responsibly!

"WINNER, WINNER, CHICKEN DINNER!*"

*The classic Vegas celebration shouted by gamblers who hit it big.

June 1, 1911

The day Las Vegas was transformed from a township and officially incorporated as a city.

At the time, it had fewer than 2,000 residents and just one gambling joint – the Golden Gate Hotel.

It was in 1821 that Spanish explorer Rafael Rivera named this part of the Nevada desert Las Vegas – Spanish for "the meadows" – after the vast fields of wild grass nourished by numerous natural springs.

Rivera, the first European to set foot in Las Vegas, was then searching for a new route from Santa Fe to Los Angeles.

Millennia ago, the Las Vegas valley was a natural oasis and home to large creatures like the Columbian mammoth.

64

The current number of casinos on the Strip*.

*As of May 2025

Since its Golden Age in the 1970s, the Strip has seen 14 major casino implosions or demolitions. These include **The Dunes** (1993, to make way for the Bellagio), **The Sands** (1996, to make way for The Venetian), **The Hacienda** (1996, to make way for Mandalay Bay), **The Desert Inn** (2001, to make way for Wynn Las Vegas and Encore), the **Tropicana** (2024, to make way for a new baseball stadium) and the **Mirage** (2024), to make way for… **see page 51!**

“

A little bit of this town goes a very long way.

”

Hunter S. Thompson,
***Fear and Loathing in Las Vegas*, 1971**

Hunter S. Thompson's infamous account of Las Vegas excess is a chaotic masterpiece that captures the city in all its surreal glory. Las Vegas is described as the “savage heart of the American dream” and as having “a mentality so grossly atavistic that a massive crime can often slip by unrecognized.” In 1998, Johnny Depp starred in the Hollywood film adaptation, a movie now considered a cult classic.

For nearly a century, the Hoover Dam – Nevada's top non-gambling attraction – has powered the bright lights of Las Vegas.

Built over seven years beginning in 1929, it remains one of the largest construction projects in U.S. history, incorporating more than 2.3 million cubic metres (approximately 3 million cubic yards) of concrete!

Its completion ensured a steady supply of water and electricity to the city, powering the casinos and attracting new residents during the Great Depression – rapidly boosting Las Vegas's economy.

Snow in Las Vegas is described as a "once-in-a-decade" event. In 2008, the city experienced its largest snowstorm of the century so far, with more than 20 cm (eight inches) blanketing the valley!

Coincidentally, the name "Nevada" – Vegas's home state – comes from the Spanish word for "snow-covered"*.

Bonanza (see page 21) has a large collection of souvenir snow globes to celebrate this fact.

*Nevada is America's driest state and also the most mountainous.

Today, Las Vegas boasts more than 150,000 hotel rooms, the highest number of any American city.

The average price per room on the Strip is around $200 (£160), and the average casino-hotel occupancy rate is approximately 83.5 per cent.

“

Las Vegas is sort of like how God would do it if he had money.

”

Steve Wynn

April 3, 1941

The day the first resort, the El Rancho Vegas, opened on the Strip, ushering in a new themed casino era in the city. It had just 63 rooms.

Within a decade, the Last Frontier, the Flamingo and the Thunderbird had opened, effectively kickstarting the Golden Age.

After the Second World War, many returning soldiers decided to settle in Las Vegas as this was one of the few places with plenty of jobs – nearly tripling the city's population between 1940 and 1950.

"Las Vegas is the most honest fake city in the world."

Frank Scoblete

The nickname "the Strip" for Las Vegas Boulevard – the city's most recognizable street – is widely credited to former Los Angeles police officer Guy McAfee, who arrived* in Las Vegas around 1939.

He likened the developing street – then known as Highway 91 – to the iconic Sunset Strip in L.A.

*Rather aptly, McAfee was fleeing L.A. after accusations of police corruption.

CHAPTER TWO

City of Sin

Step into a world where fun meets frenzy and every corner offers a new thrill.

It's a place where rules bend and the good times just keep rolling.

Ready to take a spin around the City of Sin?

November 22, 1989

The date that American billionaire Steve Wynn opened the Mirage, the first new casino in Vegas in 16 years.

Its construction ignited a mega-resort boom, with a multitude of themed casino hotels that propelled Vegas into a new family-friendly era.

“Everything and anything you want to do, you can do in Las Vegas.”

Drew Carey

The Sphinx guarding the Luxor, Las Vegas's Egyptian-themed casino-hotel, is larger than life – nearly twice the size of the original in Giza, Egypt.

Standing 33 metres (110 feet) tall, this colossal replica took 18 months to construct before its 1993 unveiling.

Casino dice in Las Vegas differ significantly from those used in household games like Monopoly. They have sharp, precisely milled corners and edges that cause the dice to tumble more erratically and settle quickly – ensuring fair, random rolls by minimizing the chance of manipulation.

The dice are made from a translucent material called cellulose acetate, making it easier to visually inspect them and ensure they haven't been tampered with.

Now you know!

Las Vegas is the Marriage Capital of the World, hosting more than 315 weddings every single day!

There are more than 50 walk-in wedding chapels in the city, the most-famous of which is the Little White Wedding Chapel.

8 Couples who said "I DO" in Vegas

1. Mickey Rooney & Ava Gardner (1942)
2. Judy Garland & Vincente Minnelli (1945)
3. Zsa Zsa Gabor & George Sanders (1949)
4. Elizabeth Taylor & Eddie Fisher (1959)
5. Mia Farrow & Frank Sinatra (1966)
6. Elvis Presley & Priscilla Beaulieu (1967)
7. Britney Spears & Jason Allen Alexander (2004)
8. Ben Affleck & Jennifer Lopez (2022)

The second* tallest Ferris wheel in the world – soaring 167 metres (550 feet) high – can be found on the Strip, opposite Caesars Palace.

A 30-minute ride offers 700 people a 360-degree view of the city.

What's its name?
The High Roller, of course.

It was the world's tallest Ferris wheel for decades – until 2021.

Created in 1959 by graphic designer Betty Willis, the iconic "Welcome to Fabulous Las Vegas" sign is a globally recognized landmark, situated about six kilometres (four miles) south of the Strip's end.

Willis gifted the copyright of the design to the city for free, aiming to create an exciting and welcoming symbol.

"The city wanted something that would identify Las Vegas and be as exciting and welcoming as they could get," Betty once said. "We put flashing lights, chasing neon and a Disney star – everything we could to put action into it. The whole theme of the sign was to make people feel welcome."

Icons of Las Vegas: Elvis Presley

Elvis Presley, the King of Rock 'n' Roll, began his Las Vegas residency on July 31, 1969, at the International Hotel (now Westgate Las Vegas Resort & Casino) in its 2,000-seat venue.

Famously, at his first show, he remarked on his nine-year absence from live audiences: "This is the first time I've worked in front of people for nine years, and it may be the last!" It wasn't. Over the next seven years, he performed 636 sold-out shows, often twice a night.

"Man, I really like Vegas."

Elvis Presley

“If you can’t spot the sucker in the first half hour at the table, then you are the sucker.”

Mike McDermott, *Rounders*, 1998

The Guitar Hotel, owned by Hard Rock Hotel & Casino, is set to open in spring 2027.

Located on the former site of the legendary Mirage, it will be the first guitar-themed casino-hotel – featuring more than 3,000 rock 'n' roll slot machines!

Standing 137 metres (450 feet) tall, the hotel is designed to resemble a giant electric Gibson guitar.

"

Don't press your luck – you might pop it*.

"

**Common Vegas expression about quitting while you're ahead – all the best gamblers do.*

Opened in 1993, the MGM Grand boasts over 6,850 rooms and a 15,800-square-metre (170,000-square-foot) casino floor. An estimated 70,000 people walk through its lobby each day.

Beyond its renowned heavyweight boxing matches, the Grand is also famous for the 13.7-metre-tall (45-foot), 50-tonne bronze lion sculpture guarding its entrance – the largest bronze sculpture in the Northern Hemisphere and a tribute to MGM's cinematic logo.

The lion's name? Leo.

1,200

The number of individual fountains in the famous Bellagio Hotel and Casino lake – a Guinness World Record!

The 366-metre-long (1,200-foot) artificial lake holds about 83 million litres (22 million gallons) of fresh water, drawn from wells beneath the Bellagio.

The hotel's legendary Fountain Show, timed to music, operates from noon to midnight every 30 minutes daily, and lasts about five minutes.

Show up early to snag a good spot right up front.

Las Vegas is, infamously, located in the middle of the desert.

The nearest cities lie a considerable distance away in every direction.

North

Reno, Nevada – 724 km (450 miles) away.

South

Phoenix, Arizona – 483 km (300 miles) away.

West

Los Angeles, California – 435 km (270 miles) away.

East

Salt Lake City, Utah – 676 km (420 miles) away.

"The first thing Bond noticed was that Las Vegas seemed to have invented a new school of functional architecture, 'The Gilded Mousetrap School' he thought it might be called, whose main purpose was to channel the customer-mouse into the central gambling trap whether he wanted the cheese or not."

Ian Fleming,
***Diamonds Are Forever*, 1956**

"True luck consists not in holding the best of the cards at the table; luckiest is he who knows just when to rise and go home."

John Milton Hay

From December 2013, Britney Spears's show, *Britney: Piece of Me* – at the AXIS at Planet Hollywood Resort & Casino – ran for four years.

Her residency was credited with launching the modern pop residency era in Vegas – paving the way for artists like Lady Gaga, Bruno Mars and Adele.

Like Elvis, Las Vegas has Seven Ages - distinct eras of transformation.

1. The Desert Oasis Age (pre-1905 – 1930)
2. The Mobster Era (1931 – late 1945)
3. The Golden Age (1946 – 1989)
4. The Mega-Resort Revolution (1990 – early 2000s)
5. The Luxury Experience (early 2000s – early 2020s)
6. The Spectacle Era (early 2020s – present)
7. The Redevelopment Phase (present)

The Golden Age

Las Vegas's "Golden Age" began in the 1940s and lasted several decades, transforming it from a Wild West outpost into a glamorous entertainment capital.

This era fuelled America's casino culture, attracting iconic performers such as Frank Sinatra, Dean Martin, Sammy Davis Jr and Elvis Presley, who headlined in lavish showrooms alongside beautiful showgirls.

The early 1960s Rat Pack era at the Sands epitomized the city's magnetic charm, solidifying its appeal for stylish celebrities and high rollers.

41.7 million

The total number of visitors to Las Vegas in 2024, making it one of the most popular cities on Earth!

Fear of the number 13: Triskaidekaphobia

Several of Las Vegas's largest hotels skip numbering a fourth or thirteenth floor. The number 13 is considered unlucky in the U.S., while the number four carries the same superstition in East Asian cultures because its pronunciation sounds like "death".

Resorts such as The Wynn, Encore, Resorts World, Aria and Mandalay Bay, which cater to mostly American and Asian clientele, follow this practice.

Fear of the number 4: Tetraphobia

Las Vegas's corporate boom began in 1959 with the opening of the famed Las Vegas Convention Centre, now spanning over 427,000 square metres (4.6 million square feet) of event space.

As the "Convention Capital of the World", the city hosts more than 22,000 annual expos – drawing six million attendees, all seeking to blend business with pleasure.

With that in mind, dating site Ashley Madison reported in 2025 that 53 per cent of attendees admitted to adultery in Las Vegas hotels, leading the city to be voted the "best place for cheating spouses".

The Las Vegas Strip isn't in Las Vegas. It's in Paradise*.

*Clark County, *Nevada contains several incorporated cities (such as Las Vegas, Henderson and North Las Vegas) and numerous unincorporated townships, including Paradise, Spring Valley, Sunrise Manor, Enterprise, Whitney and Winchester.*

April 24, 1951

The night American icon Frank Sinatra first performed in the Painted Desert Room at the brand new Desert Inn resort.

The set marked the beginning of the legendary Rat Pack era of Las Vegas, shaping the future of the Strip in its Golden Age.

71 per cent

The number of first-time tourists who gamble when they visit Las Vegas.

In 2024, the average gambling budget for visitors to Las Vegas was $820 (£670).

In 2001, Las Vegas's most successful band on the international stage, The Killers, was born.

Today, they are considered one of the biggest rock bands of the 21st century, having sold more than 30 million albums worldwide.

"I live with the ghosts of Elvis and Frank Sinatra," frontman Brandon Flowers said. "It's a magical place, the desert, and a beautiful city, even though there are a lot of things that are wrong with it."

CHAPTER THREE

Neon Paradise

Welcome to Paradise! Bellagio, Caesar's Palace, MGM Grand, The Palazzo, Cosmopolitan, Luxor, Excalibur, New York-New York or Mandalay Bay…

Where shall we go next?

The original American mobster, Benjamin "Bugsy" Siegel was a leading force behind the development of the Las Vegas Strip in the 1940s.

He named his casino, the Flamingo, after his showgirl girlfriend, Virginia Hill, who was nicknamed "the Flamingo" because of her long, skinny legs.

The Flamingo opened in December 1946, becoming the third casino to open in Vegas.

20,000

The estimated number of "exotic dancers" working within the city limits on any given week in Las Vegas.

The oldest strip club in Vegas is the Palomino Club, established in 1969. Though Peppermint Hippo is good too. Not that we've been. Ahem.

The coolest bar in Las Vegas has to be the Minus5 Icebar at the LINQ Promenade. The entire venue, from the walls and seating to the glasses you drink from, is carved entirely from ice!

The bar is maintained at a constant temperature of -5°C (23°F), and guests are provided with warm parkas and gloves upon entry to stay comfortable.

It's also a great way to escape from the Nevada heat. Try their signature cocktail, the Iceberg.

"Everybody knows about Las Vegas. It's a state of mind. Some people want to come with their kids and have a great weekend. Some people want to shop. Some people want to find hookers. Some people want to eat. Some people just want to gamble. It's a potpourri of decadence."

Michael Douglas

$21.8 billion*

The amount earned from gambling by casinos on the Strip in 2024.

Clearly, the house always wins!

*Approximately £17 billion

$39,713,982.25*

The record-breaking amount won on a Megabucks jackpot at the Excalibur Hotel & Casino on the Strip. It was won in March 2003 by Josh Ford, a 25-year-old software engineer from Los Angeles.

He had put the minimum amount required to play – $3! – into the machine. On his win he once said, "I looked away for an instant, and when I looked back, I saw the winning symbols all lined up!"

It remains the biggest slot machine jackpot in history, and a Guinness World Record.

*Approximately £31 billion

“

One day I might be driving a Mercedes, and the next day I might be sleeping in it!

”

Archie Karas

In December 1992, Greek-American gambler Archie Karas – the “Wizard of Vegas” – arrived in Sin City with just $50 (£40) in his pocket. By early 1995, he had turned this into a $40 million (£31 million) fortune playing pool, poker and dice on the Strip – a legendary streak now known as “The Run”. Karas had a passion for dice and baccarat – both games of pure chance – and by mid-1995, he had lost all his winnings.

“

What do you think the casinos are doing out here in the middle of the desert? It's all about money. It is the end result of all the bright lights, and the comp trips, and all the champagne, and free hotel suites, and all the broads and all the booze. It's all been arranged just for us to get your money. That's the truth about Las Vegas: we're the only winners. The players don't stand a chance.

”

Sam Rothstein, *Casino*, 1995

100 mm*

The average amount of rainfall the city receives in a year, spread across just 26 days or so – with the most common rainfall occurring in February.

*4 inches

Say hello to...
Vegas Vic and Vegas Vickie!

For several decades, these two iconic landmarks – the 12-metre-high (40-foot) neon cowboy and cowgirl signs – stood proudly on Fremont Street in Old Vegas.

For a long time, Vic was the world's largest mechanical neon sign, his trademark greeting – "Howdy Partner" – serving as a daily reminder of Vegas's Wild West days. The two signs were hilariously "married" in a 1994 ceremony.

While Vic still tips his hat outside, Vickie now lives inside Circa Resort's lobby bar.

35,520

The total number of slot machines on the Strip in 2024, according to Las Vegas gaming statistics.

That's roughly one for every four available hotel rooms in the city.

"The lights, the noise, the letter X. It's all designed to inflame the senses. I'm overstimulated. I've gotta get out of this town!"

Ned Flanders, "Viva Ned Flanders",
The Simpsons

Located in the desert north of the Strip, MGM Resorts' 100-megawatt solar array produces up to 90 per cent of its daytime power needs.

Comprising around 323,000 solar panels across 2.6 million square metres (640 acres), the renewable electricity production is equivalent to the power used by 27,000 average U.S. homes annually.

It supplies electricity to more than 36,000 rooms at Strip properties owned by MGM, such as the Bellagio, Aria, Mandalay Bay and the Grand, making Las Vegas one of the top clean-energy cities in the world.

"Remember, what happens in Vegas stays in Vegas. Except for herpes. That shit'll come back with you."

Sid Garner, *The Hangover*, 2009

> “Las Vegas is the only place I know where money really talks. It says, ‘Goodbye!’”

Frank Sinatra

Icons of Las Vegas: Frank Sinatra

The leader of the Rat Pack, Frank Sinatra was instrumental in establishing Las Vegas as the "Entertainment Capital of the World" in the 1950s. Alongside fellow entertainers Dean Martin, Sammy Davis Jr., Joey Bishop and Peter Lawford, Sinatra's performances at the Desert Inn and the Sands Hotel and Casino redefined what made Vegas cooler than anywhere else.

When, in May 1998, Sinatra passed away, the lights on the entire Strip were dimmed in his honour.

September 29, 2023

The day Vegas's latest technological spectacle, the Sphere, opened. This colossal spherical entertainment venue stands 112 metres (366 feet) tall, while its "Exosphere" is the world's largest LED screen, covered with more than 1.2 million programmable LED pucks.

Inside, a massive 16K resolution LED screen wraps over the 18,000-seat audience, offering an immersive visual experience that has to be seen to be believed. On opening night, rock band U2 performed the first show of their Las Vegas residency.

The future of Vegas is here – and it's the Sphere!

“This whole place feels like a distortion pedal on the mind!”

Bono, after performing with U2 at the Sphere's opening night

October 15, 1998

The day the most expensive hotel ever built (at the time) opened on the Strip. Welcome to the Bellagio!

This luxurious $1.6 billion (£1.3 billion) masterpiece was inspired by Italian art and the scenery of Lake Como, Italy. The resort is named after the village of Bellagio on Lake Como – a fitting reference to the expansive artificial lake in front of the hotel, the largest on the Strip.

The Bellagio was the first Las Vegas hotel to receive the prestigious AAA Five Diamond Award.

“

The marble was hand-picked in Italy. The chefs stolen from the highest-rated restaurants in the Michelin guide book. In the villas, for his big players, the silverware is actually gold. It’s a shoo-in for the Five Diamond Award.

”

Danny Ocean, *Ocean’s Thirteen*, 2007

The iconic Bellagio hotel was a prominent filming location for both Ocean’s Eleven *and* Ocean’s Thirteen.

EDC Las Vegas

The Electric Daisy Carnival is one of the biggest electronic dance music festivals in the world.

Held at the Las Vegas Motor Speedway, it features massive stages, glowing art installations, carnival rides and nonstop music from top DJs – all under a sky lit up with neon and fireworks.

“You can take the girl out of Vegas, but you can’t take the Vegas out of the girl.”

Charisma Carpenter

8.2 metres*

The height of the world's largest chocolate fountain, located in the Bellagio hotel's Patisserie. Designed by renowned chef Jean-Pierre Maury, the fountain circulates nearly 1,814 kg (2 tons) of chocolate per minute through six high-powered pumps.

Please note: the chocolate is for display purposes only. Boo.

*27 feet

Frank's Way

The Rat Pack, including its leader, Frank Sinatra, famously partied all night on the Strip in the 1950s. Sinatra's legendary tipple was known as "Frank's Way" and comprised of three rocks (ice cubes), two fingers of 90-proof Jack Daniel's Old No. 7 whiskey and one splash of water. Sinatra loved Jack Daniels so much that when he passed away in 1998, he was buried with a bottle of it.

July 7, 2007

The seventh day of the seventh month in 2007 was billed as the "luckiest day of the century" in Las Vegas*.

To mark the day, more than 4,400 couples tied the knot in the city, significantly higher than the typical daily average of 315. Wedding chapels across Las Vegas were booked around the clock, with some even holding mass wedding ceremonies to accommodate demand.

**In gambling, 777 is widely recognized as a winning combination in slot machine games, often triggering the jackpot.*

May 3, 1999

When The Venetian Resort Las Vegas opened, it was one of the most expensive hotels ever built at the time, costing $1.5 billion (£1.2 billion). It pioneered the all-suite concept on the Strip, offering standard rooms that were significantly larger than average.

The resort's design – inspired by the Italian city of Venice – features replicas such as the Grand Canal with gondola rides (both indoor and outdoor), St Mark's Square and stunning Renaissance architecture adorned with frescoes and marble.

Icons of Las Vegas: Celine Dion

Celine Dion's first residency at Caesars Palace, A *New Day*… (2003–2007), revolutionized Las Vegas entertainment.

Her sold-out shows proved that the Strip wasn't just for nostalgia acts – it could be home to global superstars too.

The star returned in 2011 with a second blockbuster residency, *Celine* – which ran until 2019 (with a few breaks).

Celine by Numbers

Total shows: 1,144

Total gross revenue: $681 million (£545 million)

Total attendance: More than 5 million fans

CHAPTER FOUR

Strip Tease

Throw on your feathered headdress and sequined ballgown – this is where glamour meets grit, and the lights never dim.

It's a stage where fantasy comes to life and anything can happen.

Ready to strut down the Strip?

The ten longest-surviving casinos in Las Vegas

1. Flamingo (1946)
2. SAHARA (1952)
3. Tropicana (1957)*
4. The LINQ (opened as Flamingo Capri, 1959)
5. Caesars Palace (1966)
6. Circus Circus (1968)
7. Harrah's (as Holiday Casino, 1973)
8. The Cromwell (as Barbary Coast, 1978)
9. Excalibur (1990)
10. Luxor (1993)

*Closed in April 2024

May 24, 1955

The Moulin Rouge – the first racially integrated casiono-hotel in Las Vegas (and one of the first in the U.S.) – opened on this day. Located off the Strip in the Westside neighbourhood, it quickly became a popular spot for both Black and white patrons as well as entertainers who were often excluded from other venues. The Moulin Rouge played a crucial role in the desegregation of the city.

Sammy Davis Jr. remarked about the time: "In Vegas for 20 minutes, our skin had no colour. Then the second we stepped off the stage, we were coloured again… The other acts could gamble or… have a drink, but we had to leave through the kitchen with the garbage."

“I’ve always thought of this city as Disneyland for adults… There’s no danger of Las Vegas expiring from an excess of good taste.”

Mary Jo Putney

Steve Aoki is a powerhouse in the Vegas club scene, known for his high-energy sets, wild crowd interactions and signature cake-throwing moments.

He's a resident DJ at top venues like Hakkasan and Omnia, where fans pack the dance floors for his electrifying performances.

“

Las Vegas is the only town in the world whose skyline is made up neither of buildings, like New York, nor of trees, like Wilbraham, but signs.

”

Tom Wolfe

There are no clocks or windows inside most Las Vegas casinos. The hope is that guests will lose track of time and stay longer – and keep gambling!

The environment is carefully designed to be stimulating and full of sensory cues that encourage continued play.

Often called America's most food-obsessed city, Las Vegas boasts a vibrant fine-dining and culinary scene. The city features more than 2,500 restaurants, with many considered among the best places to dine in the country.

Celebrity chef Gordon Ramsay alone has six popular restaurants on the Strip: Hell's Kitchen (Caesars Palace), Ramsay's Kitchen (Harrah's), Gordon Ramsay Steak (Paris Las Vegas), Gordon Ramsay Burger (Planet Hollywood Resort & Casino), Gordon Ramsay Pub & Grill (Caesars Palace) and Gordon Ramsay Fish & Chips (LINQ Promenade).

"You can compare the standard of food in Las Vegas to New York, London and Paris."

Gordon Ramsay

Las Vegas is known as the boxing capital of the world.

The craze for Saturday night fighting kicked off on July 22, 1963, when the first WBC Heavyweight Title match pitted Floyd Patterson against Sonny Liston at the Las Vegas Convention Centre.

Liston won by knockout just two minutes and 10 seconds into the first round.

“What happens in Vegas... gets settled in the ring.”

Poster to hype a Vegas boxing showdown

In 2023, a report revealed that the luckiest casino on the Strip was… The Mirage*.

Of all Vegas casinos, it received the highest number of TripAdvisor reviews mentioning a good luck experience.

*Possibly unrelated but The Mirage closed for good on July 15, 2024.

In Las Vegas, it is illegal to drive a camel on the highway*.

*This curious law dates back to the nineteenth century, when camels were used for transportation and construction work in the desert.

"I went to Vegas for my fortieth birthday, and my wife and I got married. It was at one of the chapels where a lot of famous people had got married, because there were pictures of all of them on the wall. I was looking round thinking, fucking hell, I'm getting married where what's-his-name got married, and so-and-so. And then, at the end, I looked round, and realized every single person on the wall had got divorced. I thought, oh shit, this isn't going to last long, then."

Michael Caine*

**Michael and his wife, Shakira, have been married for more than 50 years.*

In true Vegas fashion, tattoo shops like Club Tattoo at Planet Hollywood stay open deep into the night.

Whether you're adding to your ink collection or getting a spontaneous (neon-fuelled) first, late-night tattoos are just another unforgettable way Vegas leaves its mark – literally.

Since launching his Vegas residency in December 2016, Bruno Mars has become a staple on the Strip – mixing chart-topping hits with a dynamic stage presence.

In May 2025, he delivered his 100th show at Park MGM.

49-51 per cent

The chance of winning at blackjack, the game consistently ranked as the easiest casino game to beat.

In May 1995, Australian billionaire Kerry Packer won $20 million (£16 million) in just 40 minutes playing blackjack at the MGM Grand – one of the luckiest winning streaks ever seen in Vegas.

288

The number of years it would take a single person to spend one night in every hotel room on the Strip.

There's no such thing as beginner's luck in games of chance*.

*One of the most popular Las Vegas superstitions is that gamblers tend to win big on their first day in a casino on the Strip.

April 11, 2004

In a highly publicized gamble, British entrepreneur Ashley Revell sold all his possessions, including his house and clothes, to fund a single bet. With $135,300 (£108,000) in hand, he went to the Plaza Hotel & Casino and placed his entire wealth on a single spin at the roulette table.

The ball famously landed on red 7, instantly doubling his money to $270,600 (£216,000). Revell tipped the dealer $600 (£480) on the spot, then walked away.

**This double-or-nothing gamble later inspired a reality TV concept developed by Simon Cowell in 2011.*

5 per cent

The odds of winning a high-denomination pay-out from a Las Vegas slot machine.

Slot machines account for over 60 percent of a typical casino's annual revenue.

At Tipsy Robot in Planet Hollywood, your bartender isn't human – it's a robot!

High-tech arms mix, shake and pour cocktails with precision and flair, all while flashing lights and striking dance moves.

It's part bar, part show and 100 per cent Vegas weird.

One of the biggest celebrity "whales" – gamblers who consistently wager more than $25,000 (£20,000) per hand – in Las Vegas history is former NBA star Charles Barkley.

He claims to have lost more than $30 million (£24 million) throughout his gambling career – reporting losses of over $1 million (£800,000) in a single day between 10 and 20 times in his life.

January 13, 1906

The day Vegas's first and longest-running gambling establishment, the Golden Gate Hotel and Casino, officially opened its saloon doors.

Located at 1 Fremont Street – the very first numbered address in Downtown Las Vegas – it originally operated as the Hotel Nevada, featuring 106 rooms, until its renaming in 1955. The Golden Gate was the first Vegas building constructed from concrete and was the first place in the city to have a telephone (from 1907).

Its legendary telephone number was simply "1".

Binion's Horseshoe, now known as Binion's Gambling Hall & Hotel at 128 Fremont Street, was the first casino in Downtown Las Vegas to replace traditional sawdust-covered floors with carpeting.

Introduced by founder Benny Binion, this simple innovation significantly enhanced comfort for gamblers and quickly became a standard feature across the casino industry, contributing to the more welcoming atmosphere*.

**To gamblers, a "carpet joint" is a casino that caters to high rollers.*

“Let me set the record straight: I love Vegas. There you go. Always have.”

Barack Obama

If you visit Las Vegas, you must adventure a little further down what is known as the Extraterrestrial Highway*. Many individuals have reported UFO sightings along this 158-km (98-mile) stretch of road that runs uninterrupted through nothing but desert.

It's home to the "Black Mailbox", a famous gathering point for UFO seekers hoping to observe alien spacecraft. Some claim to have witnessed fast-moving aerial phenomena in the night sky – highly visible thanks to the minimal light pollution.

**Officially designated Nevada State Route 375*

September 24, 1980

The day William Lee Bergstrom, famously known as the "Suitcase Man", arrived at Binion's Horseshoe Casino in Las Vegas. He carried two suitcases: one empty, and the other filled with $777,000 in cash (equivalent to approximately $2.97 million – or £2.38 million – today).

Bergstrom proceeded to the craps table and placed his entire fortune on a single bet. He won, filled his empty suitcase with his doubled winnings and promptly left the casino. This remarkable feat was, at the time, the highest bet ever placed in Las Vegas.

According to casino owner Ted Binion, Bergstrom had borrowed most of the money and intended to commit suicide if he lost.

Country star Miranda Lambert brought a bold Southern flair to the Las Vegas Strip with her residency, Velvet Rodeo, at Planet Hollywood.

Launched in 2022, the show is Vegas meets Nashville – and fans love it.

CHAPTER
FIVE

Desert Oasis

Delusion, illusion, hallucination – Las Vegas might just be a mirage in the heart of the desert: a dazzling place that feels real but is, in truth, almost too good to be true.

But who cares when the fun is this unforgettable?

Nevada is home to more hot springs than any other state in the U.S. – boasting around 300.

Hot springs form when geothermally heated groundwater rises through the Earth's crust. In Nevada, these springs vary from remote desert pools to commercialized tourist hotspots.

If you spot a wild spring, take care, as it could be superheated and reach boiling temperatures.

Las Vegas's home state, Nevada – originally known as the Silver State* – is today the fourth-largest gold producer in the world, behind China, Australia and Russia.

Nevada mines about 5.5 million ounces (156,000 kg) of gold a year.

**Because Nevada was the first U.S. state to discover silver ore, in 1859.*

The Strip consumes around 20 per cent of Las Vegas's total electricity, equivalent to the daily usage of about 320,000 homes!

Before solar power was introduced on the Strip in 2021, the Wynn Casino, for example, used more than two million megawatt-hours of electricity each year, with a minimum monthly electric bill of $250,000 (£200,000)!

In 2025, the Strip celebrated 100 years of… sidewalk (pavement).

Yes, the Strip first got laid in 1925 – and it's been rock hard, and Hard Rock, ever since!

1 in 49.8 million

The odds of winning the "Megabucks" progressive slot machine jackpot in spins*.

**For comparison, the odds of an average person winning an Olympic medal are approximately 1 in 662,000.*

In April 1957, showgirl Lee Merlin was famously crowned the very first – and ultimately last – "Miss Atomic Bomb". She won wearing a swimsuit adorned with a cotton mushroom cloud!

This unique beauty pageant combined two of Las Vegas's major attractions of the time – the nearby nuclear bomb tests of the 1950s and the city's iconic showgirls. Merlin, by all accounts, was a true bombshell of a beauty.

Icons of Las Vegas: Wayne Newton

Ladies and gentlemen, the one and only "Mr. Las Vegas"! Even bigger than Sinatra and Presley, Newton is Las Vegas's most popular entertainer.

Since his first show at the Desert Inn in 1958, the singer has performed more than 30,000 shows, mostly at the Flamingo. TV host Merv Griffin once joked, "Las Vegas without Wayne Newton is like Disneyland without Mickey Mouse."

Newton's most famous songs are "Danke Schön" (1963), "Summer Wind" (1965), "Red Roses for a Blue Lady" (1965) and "Daddy, Don't You Walk So Fast" (1972).

“When you say the word Las Vegas it means something. There’s not a lot of cities where the world literally brings a picture to your mind.”

Todd Phillips

The longest-running show in the history of Las Vegas is the cabaret variety show *Les Folies Bergère*, which ran for 50 years at the Tropicana Las Vegas Hotel & Casino, from 1959 to 2009. In that time, more than 30 million fans bought tickets!

The show, inspired by the original Parisian cabaret venue from the 1870s – whose name means "pleasure house" – became famed for its sparkly costumes, ornate sets and, of course, the chorus line of topless showgirls. It also featured singers, dancers, acrobats, comedians and magicians.

“Las Vegas turns women into men and men into idiots.”

Bugsy Siegel

Icons of Las Vegas: Liberace

World-renowned virtuoso pianist and the original greatest showman, Władziu Valentino Liberace – that's "Mr. Showmanship" to you! – was the first to pioneer the concept of a concert residency in Vegas, back in 1944.

At the Las Vegas Hilton, between 1950 and 1970, Liberace became the highest-paid entertainer in the world, earning more than $50,000 a week – equivalent to $586,894 (£470,000) in 2025! – and performed more than 50,000 shows.

“I don’t give concerts. I put on a show!”

Liberace

May 20, 1964

The release date of, without a doubt, the greatest cinematic love letter to Vegas, *Viva Las Vegas*. The film stars Elvis Presley (as race car driver Lucky Jackson) and Ann Margret (as Rusty Martin, a swimming instructor).

Its famous title song features Presley crooning about a "bright light city" where "fortunes are won and lost" and "a thousand pretty women" live "devil may care". As a *Variety* review famously concluded, "The film is designed to dazzle the eye, assault the ear and ignore the brain" – much like Vegas itself.

Italy is credited with creating the word "casino", derived from its description for a "small house", with origins dating back to 1744.

In Italy, anything small and cute is suffixed with "ino", such as bambino and concertino.

*Fare una grossa vincita!**

*That's "hit the jackpot" in Italian.

The origin of the word "poker" comes from the French game *poque*, a similar card game first plyed sometime around 1834. Today, Vegas is home to the World Series of Poker, the largest poker contest in the world, played across the Horseshoe and Paris Las Vegas.

In July 2024, Jonathan Tamayo was crowned world champion after outlasting 10,000 players and going all-in to win the $10 million (£8 million) first-place prize.

In the 1970s, Lola Falana became widely known as the "Queen of Las Vegas". She rose to become the city's highest-paid female performer, reportedly earning $100,000 (£80,000) per week during her groundbreaking residency at the Aladdin.

Her success as a pioneering African-American headliner was so profound that it rivalled Elvis Presley's iconic 1970s Vegas comeback. As she once famously stated, "As a kid, I dreamed of being tall, with a nice figure, and of being a dancer at the opera. Seems I took a wrong turn somewhere. But, I have no regrets!"

9,982

The number of calories* in the "quadruple bypass burger", the infamous item on the menu at the Heart Attack Grill.

Here, waitresses – dressed in revealing uniforms – are referred to as "nurses", and orders are written down as prescriptions. Diners don hospital gowns, and if they weigh more than 158 kg (350 pounds), they dine for free!

Those who do not finish their meal are punished by the nurses with a paddle-spanking. Only in Vegas.

**Five times more than a man's recommended daily allowance.*

On November 24, 1989, just nine hours after its grand opening, The Mirage casino celebrated its first Megabucks jackpot winner. Elmer Sherwin, a 76-year-old local retiree, famously won $4.6 million (£3.7 million) after reportedly playing the machine for 90 minutes – using $20 borrowed from his ex-wife, Florence.

At a press conference, Sherwin jested that Florence still wouldn't take him back. Her reported retort became part of the lore: "He said that, not me!"

The pair never remarried.

Vigorish

Often simply called "the vig" or "the juice", this is the cut a casino or bookmaker takes on every bet made. The word's roots trace back to the Yiddish *vigrish*, meaning "winnings".

Bookmakers build a small fee right into the betting odds they offer. In poker games, the casino takes a "rake" – a percentage from each pot. For other table games, such as baccarat, the casino profits from the "house edge", which is a mathematical advantage built into the game's rules and payouts.

Ultimately, the house *always* wins.

One-armed Bandit

An affectionate term for a slot machine

On August 20, 1964, The Beatles played their only Las Vegas performances – enjoying a hard day's night with two sold-out shows for over 17,000 fans at the Convention Centre.

On the morning of their performance, The Beatles were confined to the Sahara Hotel's Suite 2344 due to thousands of desperate fans. Hotel managers famously brought two slot machines to the suite so the band could try their luck at gambling.

In Vegas,
$1,000 is called
a dime.

A nickel is $500.

35 to 1

The odds of winning a single-number bet at roulette in Vegas. One of the city's most popular table games, roulette takes its name from the French word meaning "little wheel" and evolved from earlier European games like the Italian biribi.

If you're playing, number 17 is a common choice, popular for its central position on the betting layout. Many gamblers mistakenly believe the ball will land on this "sweet spot", despite all numbers having equal odds on the wheel.

There is a popular Vegas cocktail aptly called "the Las Vegas". Let's make it…

Place 45ml (1.5 oz) of Jack Daniel's and 45ml (1.5 oz) of Martini Bianco vermouth in a cocktail shaker with ice. Shake well and strain into a highball glass filled with ice.

Top up the glass with 45ml (1.5 oz) of lemonade and 45ml (1.5 oz) of Coca-Cola.

Garnish with a slice of lime.

One sip of this drink and your odds of winning increase significantly*.

**Not legally guaranteed*

Vegas Playlist

Leaving Las Vegas? This playlist will help you remember the good times – anytime!

1. "Viva Las Vegas" – Elvis Presley
2. "Leaving Las Vegas" – Sheryl Crow
3. "Sin City" – AC/DC
4. "Queen of Las Vegas" – The B-52s
5. "Let's Go to Vegas" – Faith Hill
6. "Ooh Las Vegas" – Gram Parsons
7. "Atomic City" – U2
8. "Welcome to Fabulous Las Vegas" – Brandon Flowers
9. "Pretty Vegas" – INXS
10. "Las Vegas Nights" – Hootie & the Blowfish

August 5, 1966

The date Vegas's Caesars Palace opened to much fanfare.

Themed after the Roman Empire, this venue has been the site of many of Sin City's most infamous moments: Evel Knievel's notorious motorcycle jump over its fountains in 1967; Muhammad Ali's match against Larry Holmes in 1980; the Caesars Palace Grand Prix in 1981; and Céline Dion's record-setting residency at the Colosseum, which began in 2003 – the most successful concert residency of all time.

The name of gambling's casino table game, craps, is widely believed to be borrowed from the French *crapaud*, meaning "toad".

This funny little name is thought to reference the game's early street-style origins, where players would crouch over as they played, resembling toads.

For crap shooters, the lucky number 7 is a win while numbers 2, 3 or 12 are, well, the crappiest.

All-in

When a player places all their remaining chips into the pot.

If the player wins, or holds the best hand, they take everything in the pot.

If they don't, they're out.

CHAPTER
SIX

Viva Las Vegas

From neon-soaked nights to high-stakes thrills, Las Vegas is loud, proud and unapologetically over-the-top.

This isn't just a city, it's a performance. So, raise your glass, the headliner has arrived.

All together now – "Viva Las Vegas!"

March 19, 1931

This day marked a pivotal moment for Nevada and, by extension, Las Vegas: it was the day the state legalized gambling, making it the first in the U.S. to fully embrace it.

J.G. Scrugham, then a prominent figure, famously wrote of the decision: "Nevada is embarking upon an era of what may be termed "legalized liberality" – a remarkably precise definition of what Vegas would become. This bold move came during the Great Depression, when the U.S. was grappling with severe economic hardship.

“

Las Vegas looks the way you’d imagine heaven must look at night.

”

Chuck Palahniuk

To see the world's largest gold nugget on public display – and the largest ever found with a metal detector – head to the lobby of the legendary Golden Nugget hotel and casino in downtown Las Vegas.

Known as the "Hand of Faith", this massive nugget weighs 27.2 kg (875 troy ounces / 60.7 pounds). It was discovered in 1980, in Victoria, Australia, by Kevin Hillier, and its history includes a curious twist: just 12 days before his find, Hillier had a vivid dream of unearthing a large piece of gold, inspiring him to buy a metal detector. The nugget's original sale price was just over $1 million, though it is now valued at several million dollars.

$87.7 billion*

The total economic income in 2024 from Las Vegas's tourism industry, generated through visitor spending – including gaming, accommodation, food and entertainment.

*Approximately £67.5 billion

On average, Las Vegas receives around 800,000 visitors every single week of the year!

The future arrived in Vegas first! The Vegas Loop is a super-fast underground tunnel system transporting passengers in Tesla vehicles. The initial Convention Centre Loop officially opened in April 2021, demonstrating it can move more than 32,000 passengers daily during major conventions, and cutting travel time from 25 minutes to two.

Approved plans detail 104 stations and 109 km (68 miles) of tunnels, connecting major Strip resorts, Harry Reid International Airport, Allegiant Stadium and Downtown Las Vegas. Several hotels, including Resorts World, Westgate and Encore, are already part of this expanding network.

"Vegas means comedy, tragedy, happiness and sadness all at the same time."

Artie Lange

Las Vegas boasts a surprisingly vibrant antiques scene, especially in its historic Arts District and Antique Alley. These areas are home to a variety of antique shops and markets, offering everything from mid-century furniture to vintage Vegas memorabilia.

“

I worry about Las Vegas schools. I hear in math, they only teach them to count to 21.

”

David W. Toll

Eight in every 10 visitors to Las Vegas are from the U.S. making the city the most popular American destination… for Americans.

“Viva Las Vegas, baby! Yeah!”

Austin Powers, *Austin Powers: International Man of Mystery*, 1997

"Las Vegas is one of the rare places where an acrobat, a clown, a dancer and so forth, might be able to do things like buy a house, raise a family and otherwise enjoy a regular paycheque."

Brett Martin

From Penn & Teller to David Copperfield, Siegfried & Roy to Lance Burton, and Criss Angel to Mat Franco, Las Vegas has long been the dazzling home of the world's greatest magicians and illusionists.

Criss Angel's *Mindfreak* show at Planet Hollywood is one of the most innovative magic acts in Vegas history, featuring a groundbreaking levitation trick – where, in the grand finale, Angel appears to fly around the theatre!

“No one thinks Las Vegas is real; it is illusion, but visitors willingly suspend disbelief and pretend.”

Hal Rothman

To experience the “real” Las Vegas, head to Downtown’s iconic Fremont Street – home to many of the city’s original hotels and casinos. This historic area predates the Strip, and features vintage legends such as Binion’s, the Fremont Hotel, the Golden Nugget and the city’s longest-running casino, Golden Gate Hotel and Casino.

Today, the area is renowned for the Fremont Street Experience, a pedestrian mall crowned by Viva Vision, the world’s largest video screen. Spanning five blocks and powered by over 49 million LED lights, it lives up to its nickname – the Glitter Gulch.

Icons of Las Vegas: David Copperfield

A true Vegas legend, magician David Copperfield performs hundreds of shows a year at the MGM Grand.

Known for his mind-blowing illusions, emotional storytelling and classic stagecraft, he holds the title of the most successful solo entertainer in history.

17,538.8

The total casino floor space, in square metres*, of the largest Las Vegas casino – the Wynn/Encore Resort and Casino. It boasts more than 1,962 slot machines and 137 table games.

If you're heading to Wynn's, make sure to stop and watch the *Lake of Dreams* show, the free, open-air spectacle that operates every half-hour from dusk. Incredible!

**118,786 square feet*

Three Hours

The average amount of time a visitor spends gambling each day of their visit. Most trips to Vegas last around four days.

If you're a low roller, head first to the $5 slot machines – the games with the highest pay-outs in Vegas.

Las Vegas is the third-hottest city in America.

In the summer of 2024, the city recorded its hottest day ever, with temperatures soaring to a scorching 120°F (49°C).

At such blistering temperatures, you could even fry an egg on a car bonnet.

Shortly after its 2009 opening, the Strip's Vdara Hotel & Spa earned its infamous nickname, the "Death Ray Hotel". The building's curved, reflective façade acted like a giant magnifying glass, focusing the sun's rays onto a "hot spot" on the pool deck. This concentrated heat reached temperatures high enough to singe hair, melt plastic cups and burn skin.

Though management referrred to it as a "solar convergence phenomenon", the "death ray" moniker stuck. The hotel eventually mitigated the issue by applying anti-reflective film to its windows.

There are scores of iconic thrill-rides and rollercoasters in Las Vegas.

The big daddy of them all has to be the SlotZilla, a 12-storey, slot-machine-themed zipline that sees visitors soar 518 metres (1,700 feet) through the sky at speeds of up to 56 km/h (35 mph) over the Fremont Street Experience canopy of shops.

Welcome to… The Strat!

No, it's not another guitar-themed hotel. It's a stratospheric tower that soars 350 metres (1,149 feet) into the sky, the tallest free-standing observation structure in the entire U.S.

Built in 1996, the tower offers the best panoramic views of the Strip and the surrounding desert landscape.

With over four billion streams on Spotify, The Weeknd's "Blinding Lights" is the platform's most streamed song of the twenty-first century.

The artist, Abel Tesfaye, explained the song's inspiration: "It's about driving through Las Vegas... blinded by streetlights, and nothing could stop you from trying to go see that person, because you're so lonely."

While the lyrics convey a broader emotional state, the song's iconic music video is famously set in Las Vegas, making it one of the most prominent cultural associations with the city in recent music.

The word “jackpot” originated in nineteenth-century poker, where the pot could only be won if a player held a pair of jacks or better.

If no one had such a hand, the pot would carry over, growing with each round. When someone finally claimed the pot, it was called a “jackpot”. Since then, the term has evolved to mean any big money prize or sudden cash windfall.

Many casinos on the Strip feature outrageously ornate carpet patterns that, if stared at for too long, can make gamblers feel queasy.

This is entirely intentional: the designs encourage players to keep their gaze upwards, focused on the games. They also help camouflage spills from drinks, vomit and fallen gambling chips.

The MGM Grand's is famously over-the-top.

One of the world's most successful DJs, Tiësto is a true pioneer behind the EDM takeover in Las Vegas. With long-running residencies at clubs like Hakkasan, Omnia and Zouk, he has helped transform the Strip into a global dance music capital.

Known for his high-energy sets and massive festival vibes, Tiësto continues to draw packed crowds every weekend.

“

When I travelled with Frank Sinatra, God rest his soul, I used to drink like I could do it. In Vegas, the Rat Pack, which I was a little part of, drank all night and slept most of the day. Then, about 5 o’clock, we’d meet in the hotel steam room, lock the door, and steam our brains out.

”

Don Rickles

"America is a very poor lens through which to view Las Vegas, while Las Vegas is a wonderful lens through which to view America."

David Hickey

July 15, 2004

The day the legendary Las Vegas Monorail first began shuttling people about, providing a vital transportation link along the east side of the Strip.

This 6.3-km (3.9-mile) automated monorail offers visitors an efficient way to travel between major casinos and attractions. It features seven stations: MGM Grand, Horseshoe/Paris Las Vegas, Flamingo/Caesars Palace, Harrah's/The LINQ, Boingo Station at the Las Vegas Convention Centre, Westgate Las Vegas and SAHARA Las Vegas Station.

Since opening, it has transported more than 106 million passengers, significantly reducing traffic on the Strip.

Icons of Las Vegas: Adele

Launched in 2022, Adele's "Weekends with Adele" residency at Caesars Palace has revitalized Vegas entertainment.

The star's emotionally charged performances blend powerhouse vocals with candid storytelling and dry British humour – making her one of the Strip's most refreshing headliners in recent years.

Las Vegas is widely considered the "Gambling Capital of America". This reputation for large-scale gaming and entertainment has inspired similar nicknames globally.

Outside the U.S., Romania's Bucharest is known as the "Las Vegas of Europe" while Blackpool, a UK seaside town with its famous promenade and illuminations, is referred to as the "Las Vegas of the North".

Perhaps most significantly, Macau is now globally recognized as the "Las Vegas of the East", having surpassed the Strip for the first time in 2019 in terms of gambling revenue.

Las Vegas is so bright that it's one of the most visible spots on Earth from space.

Thanks to its intense concentration of lights along the Strip, astronauts aboard the International Space Station have often noted how the city glows brilliantly against the dark desert.

“

I love Las Vegas.
No clocks. No locks.
No restrictions.

”

Marlene Dietrich